Facing forward

The CAFOD/Christian Aid/DLT Lent Book 2006

Small diamonds may sparkle brightly, and these short quotes from Samuel Rutherford shine with the beauty of Christ. We appreciate the sweet light of such gems all the more when we understand that Rutherford found them in the dark mines of sorrow.

Joel R. Beeke
President, Puritan Reformed Theological Seminary,
Grand Rapids, Michigan

When I first stumbled upon Samuel Rutherford, I knew I had encountered a man who knew Christ. Ever since I have devoured Rutherford's writing and sermons as fuel for my own spiritual fire. His enjoyment and intimate knowledge of our risen Lord has encouraged the same in me. Christian Focus has served the church well with this small volume of collected quotes from Rutherford. Be prepared to encounter soul-encouraging thoughts that will direct you to a soul-loving Saviour.

Jason Helopoulos
Senior Pastor, University Reformed Church, East Lansing,
Michigan
Author, *A Neglected Grace: Family Worship in the Christian Home
and Covenantal Baptism*

A fascinating introduction, a beautiful collection of quotes, and a wealth of profound truth, this book is a superb introduction to the life and theology of Samuel Rutherford. If you have never encountered Rutherford before, this is an excellent place to start, and if you know Rutherford well, this is a wonderful place to meet him again. This book is a great reminder of the achievements of his life, the beauty of his writings, and above all, the glory of his Saviour. Reading the book won't take you long, but meditating on the words will continue for a lifetime.

Thomas Davis
Minister, Carloway Free Church, Isle of Lewis, Scotland

For those who are newly acquainted with Samuel Rutherford, Malcolm Maclean's introduction opens a window into the person and theology of arguably the most prominent theologian of the Scottish Second Reformation. It shows Rutherford's distinct devotion to Christ and his love for fellow saints. Furthermore, Malcolm's selection and categorisation of Rutherford's writings provides us with a clear roadmap into Rutherford's mind, which I trust would prove helpful even to those who are familiar with his works. I would heartily recommend this book to all who seek to know more about Samuel Rutherford and Scottish theology.

Song-En Poon
Pastor, Reformed Bible Presbyterian Church, Singapore

This is a delightfully enjoyable introduction to one of the greatest of all Scotsmen, Samuel Rutherford. Soon his entire Works are going to be published in the USA. Two volumes were written in Latin and have never been translated. This indicates the growing world-wide interest in Rutherford today. There is no better place to begin to understand him than this book, beginning with its living introduction. Then consider slowly this magnificent selection of the most vivid and memorable quotations of Rutherford which make up the bulk of the book. You may be familiar with the work of Anne Ross Cousin, a Scottish pastor's wife, who delighted in Rutherford and was inspired to write a poem that originally was a couple of dozen verses in length. It has been abbreviated into a much loved hymn that begins, 'The sands of time are sinking.' In fact we sang it at my wife's funeral. Rutherford does that for the reader. He makes you think. He gives you fresh joy and hope. Just jump into him anywhere in this book and read! Then read his wonderful collection of letters. He makes God lovingly real and near and beautiful.

Geoffrey Thomas
Conference Speaker and author, Aberystwyth, Wales

The Fiery Edge of Love

A Collection of Quotes from Samuel Rutherford

CHRISTIAN
HERITAGE

Copyright © Christian Focus Publications 2021

Hardback ISBN 978-1-5271-0727-4
Ebook ISBN 978-1-5271-0849-3

10 9 8 7 6 5 4 3 2 1

First published in 2021
in the Christian Heritage imprint
by
Christian Focus Publications Ltd,
Geanies House, Fearn, Ross-shire,
IV20 1TW, Great Britain

www.christianfocus.com

Cover by Rubner Durais

Printed by Gutenberg, Malta

CONTENTS

INTRODUCTION

The life of Samuel Rutherford reveals an extraordinary man who excelled in a variety of activities. Such was his brilliance that it is impossible to classify him under one area. He was a preacher of renown, an ecclesiastic with inflexible convictions, a writer of devotional works that carry the touch of heaven, a theologian prepared to go as far as his reason could take him, an advocate of political ideas that few at that time dared to commit to print and which would have cost him his life had he survived to be put on trial, and a contributor to the production of the Westminster Confession of Faith and Catechisms, documents that have expressed the Christian faith of millions.

The passing of time has dimmed the awareness of his brilliance to some extent. His original sermons contain words and phrases no longer in common use, his contribution to political thought has long been forgotten, his ecclesiastical convictions about the unity of the church have been made almost irrelevant by the numerous divisions of today, his theological writings lie buried in Latin, and few who adhere to the Westminster Confession and Catechisms have any idea about the men who produced them. But his collected letters and edited volumes of sermons remain, and several biographies and other studies of him are available, and they reveal a lot about the man.[1]

HIS LIFE (1660-61)

Born in 1600, Rutherford was to live through a tumultuous period in British national life. The Union of the Crowns of Scotland and England took place when he was a child, in 1603, but it would be another century before the Union of their Parliaments occurred. While James VI was the legal successor to Elizabeth I of England as monarch, it was also assumed that he would stabilise the Protestant cause in Britain. His departure from Edinburgh to London produced some important consequences, such as the appearance of the King James Version of the Bible. Nevertheless, his reign, and the reign of his son Charles I, caused instability in the Scottish church, mainly because of their desire to have Episcopacy as the national religion.

---

1   See list of biographies in the Appendix.

Rutherford was born in Nisbet, a village in the Scottish Borders, into a farming family of some means.[2] After attending school in nearby Jedburgh, he went to Edinburgh University and received his MA in 1621. In 1623, he was appointed Regent of Humanity at the University (where he taught Latin and literature).

Two years later, in 1625, Rutherford was forced to leave the university because of a personal scandal connected to his relationship with Eupham Hamilton, who was about to become his first wife. If the scandal involved immorality, as some claim was the case, it is very surprising that he was accepted as a Christian minister in 1627. And as some biographers point out, in later years when Rutherford was involved in several controversies, 'no reference appears to have ever been made to this, by his most relentless adversaries.'[3] If the problem had been serious, surely it would have been mentioned in such contexts.

It is not clear when Samuel became a Christian. The earliest reference in his letters to a possible time is found in one he wrote in July 1636 to Lady Kenmure when he says about his banishment to Aberdeen that it was 'that honour that I have prayed for these sixteen years'; sixteen years before 1636 was 1620, when he would have

---

2   According to A. Taylor Innes, Samuel's usual spelling of his surname was Rutherfurd (p. 6).

3   Murray, pp. 18-22; Thomson, p. 13.

been nineteen or twenty.[4] That reference indicates that he was aware then of the possibility of persecution as a Christian, and indicates that he was already a believer.

If his conversion occurred around or before 1620, then the scandal in 1625 could have been one of spiritual redirection concerning his path in life. Gilmour says that it is almost certain that Rutherford began to study theology in 1625 after leaving his position in the university. The theological course lasted for two years, which explains why he was ready to begin his ministry in Anwoth in 1627.[5]

His ministry in Anwoth was to last for nine years, from 1627 to 1636. In addition to serving his own congregation, he preached in other places and so became well known in the area, with one outcome being that many made the journey regularly to hear him at Anwoth. Rutherford experienced deep personal sorrow during his time in Anwoth. His wife passed away in 1630 after an illness of thirteen months, and before then they had lost their two children. Soon after the passing of his wife, his mother who had come to live with him also died.

---

4   William Campbell (1958), *The Triumph of Presbyterianism*, Saint Andrew Press, 73. Vol. 1, p. 7. He suggests that the letter refers to Rutherford's conversion or to a call to the ministry.

5   Gilmour, pp. 28-30.

Those years were ones of difficulty for the church in Scotland due to ecclesiastical attempts to redefine the structures and activities of the Presbyterian church, and Rutherford was not the man to ignore those attempts. In 1636, a book in Latin by Rutherford against Arminianism[6] had been published in Amsterdam and this work raised the ire of his ecclesiastical opponents in Scotland. His ministry in Anwoth ceased in July of that year when an ecclesiastical body in Edinburgh, the High Commission, exiled him to Aberdeen, an exile which lasted for about two years. During this period, he wrote many letters to colleagues in the ministry, to his congregation and to other friends, including members of the aristocracy. They were later collected with other of his letters and published.

Circumstances changed for the better in 1638, the year in which the National Covenant was signed, and he was able to return to his congregation in Anwoth. His time there was to be short because the Church of Scotland moved him to St Andrews in 1639 as Professor of Divinity at St Mary's College. Rutherford was reluctant to go and only agreed to do so when he was assured that he would be able to preach regularly in the town church along with its minister Robert Blair.

---

6   The book was entitled *Exercitationes Apologeticae pro Divina Gratia*.

Soon after he moved to St Andrews, Rutherford married again, his new wife being Jean McMath. They were to have seven children, but only one, a daughter called Agnes, was to survive him. Rutherford moved there in 1643 as one of the Scottish Commissioners who participated in the Westminster Assembly, the gathering of pastors and scholars that produced the Westminster Confession of Faith and the Larger and Shorter Catechisms. Rutherford was to be in London for four years and during that time, in addition to his contributions at the Assembly, he also wrote and published several books. One of them, *Lex, Rex*, was a volume on political theory, published in 1644, and in it he argued for a limited royal authority, including the idea that the power of a monarch was given to him by the consent of the people rather than by divine right, and that it was appropriate and right for the people to resist tyranny.[7]

Rutherford returned to St Andrews in 1647 and shortly afterwards he became Principal of St Mary's. In 1648, he was invited to take a chair of theology in a Dutch university, and three years later he was invited to a similar position in Utrecht. In that same year, in 1651,

---

7   An interesting study of the ideas of Rutherford is found in David Field's chapter in *Tale of Two Cities*, published in 2005 by IVP. Field's chapter is called 'Put not your Trust in Princes – Samuel Rutherford, the four causes, and the limits of civil government.'

he became the Rector of the University in St Andrews. He was now recognised as a theologian of European stature.

Life, however, was marred for Rutherford by the controversy in Scotland between Resolutioners and Protestors, the former being willing to accept the future Charles II's agreement to follow the requirements of the Solemn League and Covenant, whereas the latter were against his involvement because of his unreliable character. The division separated friends, including Rutherford and Blair. Yet Rutherford never moved from his Protestor convictions in this matter.

In 1660, the Stuart monarchy was restored after the death of Oliver Cromwell and Charles II became king. It was expected that those who opposed his family and his regime would be targeted. In the autumn of that year, Rutherford's volume on political theory, *Lex, Rex*, was condemned by the Scottish Parliament and copies of it were burned in Edinburgh and St Andrews.

The following spring, he was summoned to appear before the Scottish Parliament on the charge of treason. When its representatives went to inform him, they discovered that Rutherford was dying. He responded to their message with words that have stirred many as they read them: 'Tell them that I have a summons already before a superior judge and judicatory, and I behove to answer my first summons; and ere your day come, I will be where few kings and great folks come.'

Samuel Rutherford died on the morning of March 29, 1661. His final evening had been marked by wonderful expressions of faith pouring out of the lips of the dying Christian. Mr Blair, who was present, asked him: 'What think ye now of Christ?' Rutherford replied: 'I shall live and adore Him. Glory! glory to my Creator and my Redeemer for ever! Glory shines in Immanuel's land.' Later that day he said: 'Oh! that all my brethren in the land may know what a Master I have served, and what peace I have this day. I shall sleep in Christ, and when I awake I shall be satisfied with His likeness. This night shall close the door, and put my anchor within the veil; and I shall go away in a sleep by five of the clock in the morning.' And he spoke true.

HIS FAME

Although Rutherford is known largely today because of his letters, which we will consider below in the next section, those who knew him also esteemed his preaching and pastoral abilities and his theological understanding. He was known as a powerful preacher who delighted in commending Jesus Christ. Alexander Whyte, in his assessment of Marion McNaught, one of Rutherford's correspondents, records her opinion of Rutherford: 'I go to Anwoth so often because, though other ministers show me the majesty of God and the plague of my own heart, Mr. Samuel does both these things, but he also shows me, as no other minister ever does, the loveliness of Christ.'[8]

Her assessment was shared by many others. There is the often-told story of the English merchant who visited Scotland and heard three famous preachers. At St Andrews, he heard a sweet, majestic-looking man (Robert Blair) who showed him the majesty of God; at Irvine he heard David Dickson who showed the merchant his own heart; at Anwoth he heard a little fair man (Samuel Rutherford) who showed him the loveliness of Christ. Another who heard Rutherford preach wrote: 'Many times I thought he would have flown out of the pulpit when he came to speak of Jesus Christ; but he was never in his right element but when he was commending Him.'[9]

Rutherford was also known for his pastoral commitment. What was it like? We can turn to Loane for a summary: 'His early rising, his tireless studies, his constant labours, his patient vigils, all had this goal in view. He was possessed with the Shepherd's watchful eye for those that were in trouble, and the Saviour's tender heart for all who were yet out of the way. The herd-boys were not too humble for him to seek out and

---

8   Whyte, pp. 26-27

9   Gilmour, pp. 40-42.

instruct; the high-born were not too lofty for him to wait on and rebuke. He yearned over those who were still unsaved with a love and longing which were akin to the passion for souls that wrung the heart of Christ himself…. His thoughts by day and dreams by night were all centred on the needs of his flock, and there were times when sleep fled from his eyes in his anxiety for the lambs of his fold.'[10]

Moreover, as we have already noticed, Rutherford was a profound theologian. The fact that he was chosen as one of the Scottish delegates to the famous Westminster Assembly which produced the Westminster Confession and Catechisms tells us that he was a most capable scholar. James Walker, in his *The Theology and Theologians of Scotland*, refers to Rutherford's scholastic tendency; in fact, he calls Rutherford 'the greatest scholastic of our Presbyterian Church'.[11] Loane's assessment helps us understand something of the greatness of Rutherford: 'No-one in Scotland ranked so high as preacher or scholar, and it was the home of both. No-one in England was his master in theology or controversy, and it was an age of giants. The world has seldom seen a union of scholastic

---

10   Loane, p. 54.

11   James Walker (1872), *The Theology and Theologians of Scotland*, T. and T. Clark, p. 12.

genius and spiritual devotion equal to that which he displayed.'[12]

As indicated already, Rutherford was also a notable author. He wrote thirteen works of theology. In addition to his political work *Lex, Rex*, he produced books on ecclesiastical practice defending Presbyterianism, books on theological issues such as his study on the covenant of works and the covenant of grace or his work on the matter of issues of conscience, and books on the person and work of Christ and on Christian discipleship. In addition, he wrote scholarly works in Latin on Arminianism and on Providence.[13] He had intended to write commentaries on Isaiah and Hosea, but they do not seem to have been written, or if they were, they have been lost.[14]

Today, he is best known for his letters.

HIS LETTERS

Various editions of the letters have been published: the first was in Holland in 1664 by Rutherford's former student Robert McWard under the title *Joshua Redivivus*, primarily for those who were facing or would

---

12 Loane, p. 86.

13 See list of his writings at close of this chapter.

14 Thomson, p. 43.

face persecution.[15] The title suggests that Rutherford functioned in a manner similar to Joshua when he went to spy out the land of Canaan. The letters are Rutherford's report of the way God dealt with him. He alludes to this function in one of his letters: 'But He would send me as a spy into this wilderness of suffering, to see the land and try the ford; and I cannot make a lie of Christ's cross. I can report nothing but good both of Him and it, lest others should faint.'

Some have difficulty reconciling his letters with several of his writings, such as *Lex, Rex*, because his letters reveal a devotional life not seen in these other works. As can be seen from Rutherford's self-description, 'but I am made of extremes', made in a letter to David Dickson (168),[16] he was aware of this trait in his personality. But his awareness of that character trait does not justify extending the trait to his ecclesiastical and political writings as if they were its sinful expression and his letters its sanctified expression. Rutherford may

---

15   This edition contained 284 letters. Other letters were added to subsequent editions. The letters number 365 in the Bonar edition, the edition that is available today: of them, 65 were written before Rutherford's exile to Aberdeen (1627-36), 220 from exile in Aberdeen (1636-38), and the remainder after his release from exile (1638-61). Bonar's edition, which was the thirtieth, seems to be the first to place the letters in chronological order. Other letters have been discovered as well.

16   Numbers in parenthesis are to the letters in Bonar's edition.

have been wrong in his political conclusions, but his writings were the practical expression of one who firmly believed that Scotland was in covenant with Christ, a relationship that demanded or justified certain national expressions. It was his love for Christ that motivated his actions, including his writings.

Many object to his letters because of his erotic language when describing the relationship between Christ and His Church corporately or Christ and individual believers. For example, Rutherford writes: 'I confidently believe there is a bed made for Christ and me, and that we shall take our fill of love in it' (165); 'I have a love-bed with Christ, and am filled with his love' (264). Yet this imagery was not unique to Rutherford; it is found in other writers of the seventeenth century. William Campbell states that this usage was technical, 'springing from the conception of Church as the Bride of Christ and from an allegorical interpretation and use of the Song of Solomon'.[17] John Macleod in his *Scottish Theology* says: 'When exception is taken to them on the ground that they use so freely the language of nuptial love, the critics, to be justified in their fault-finding, ought first to expunge from Scripture the Song of Songs, the 45th Psalm, and much of the language in the Prophets and in the New Testament which speak of the

---

17   Campbell, p. 75.

Lord as espoused to His Church and of the Church as His Bride.'[18]

It is worth noting that Rutherford also used other images, for example, from banking practices: 'Dear brother, help me, a poor debtor, to pay the interest; for I cannot come nigh to pay the interest' (110). He was also prepared to use his own physical frame to illustrate his spiritual situation:'My short legs could not step over this lair, or sinking mire; and, therefore, my Lord Jesus will bear me through' (110).

His letters were regarded from the first as being of great spiritual benefit. The fact that Bonar's edition contains 365 letters points to its use as a daily devotional for a year. Philip comments regarding the letters:'The whole circle of Christian life, its difficulties, its duties, its hopes, the heights and depths of faith and experience, everything that belongs to the Gospel and to its challenge, to holiness and its fruition, to the rightful recognition of God and to the understanding of the unsearchable riches of Christ, are spoken of with insight and passion and with a force that is compelling.'[19]

In his letters, Rutherford alludes to many doctrines. I will mention six that stand out clearly. *First, Rutherford was committed to the sovereignty of God.* His appreciation

---

18   John Macleod (1943), *Scottish Theology*, Knox Press, pp. 68-69.

19   Adam Philip (nd), *The Devotional Literature of Scotland*, James Clarke, p. 122.

of this doctrine included divine sovereignty in salvation, but in the letters the main emphasis is God's sovereignty in providence. He realised that it was important for a believer to submit to God's chastisements. Marion McNaught was exhorted to 'welcome every rod of God, for I find not in the whole book of God a greater note of the child of God, than to fall down and kiss the feet of an angry God' (12). Lady Kenmure was reminded that 'these many years the Lord hath been teaching you to read and study well the book of holy, holy, and spotless sovereignty, in suffering from some nigh-hand, and some far off. Whoever be the instruments, the replying of clay to the Potter, the Former of all, is unbeseeming the nothing-creature' (347).

Rutherford personally experienced several difficult providences, yet maintained his faith in God. When his first wife died, he wrote, 'My wife now, after long disease and torment, for the space of a year and a month, is departed this life. The Lord hath done it; blessed be His name' (11). He drew lessons from these experiences that he used when helping others in similar situations. To one of his parishioners, Mrs Taylor, who had lost her son, he wrote: 'I was in your Condition. I had but two children, and both are dead since I came hither. The supreme and absolute Father of all things giveth not an account of any of his matters. The good husbandman may pluck his roses, and gather in his lilies in midsummer….and he may transplant young trees out of the lower ground to the higher…. What is that to you or me? The goods are his own' (310).

Second, Rutherford was captivated by Jesus Christ. He draws great comfort from Christ's life and atoning death, from His activity in heaven in the present and from His interaction with His people, individually and corporately, at His second coming. Rutherford had a profound understanding of the person and work of Christ, and for all his use of dramatic imagery to describe Christ he does not fall into theological departure from the historic creedal statements regarding Christ. Yet his response to Christ was not merely at an intellectual level; it is clear from his letters that he was passionately in love with Jesus. And his relationship with Christ was a developing one. To David Dickson he wrote, 'I never before came to that degree or pitch of communion with Christ that I have now attained to' (110). To John Gordon of Rusco, Rutherford wrote: 'Brother, I may, from new experience, speak of Christ to you. Oh, if ye saw in Him what I see! A river of God's unseen joys has flowed from bank to brae over my soul since I parted with you' (147).

Third, the reality of heaven contributed to Rutherford's spirituality. He regularly refers to heaven both as an encouragement and as a stimulus for dedication. Heaven will make up for the difficulties endured on earth. Heaven is God's reward. But it is heaven with Christ (246, 247). When preaching to the House of Commons he had exclaimed: 'O for Eternity's leisure to look on Him, to feast upon a sight of His face! O for the long summer day of endless ages to stand beside Him and enjoy Him! O time, O sin, be removed out of the way! O day, fairest of days, dawn.'[20] Heaven meant a great deal to Rutherford and he refers to aspects of it throughout his letters.

Fourth, Rutherford constantly expresses a love for the church. He reminds his correspondents to pray for the church (for example, he writes to Lady Kenmure: 'I trust also, Madam, that ye will be careful to present to the Lord the present estate of this decaying kirk' [3]). He can sound like an Old Testament prophet as he pictures the state of the church: 'I see the Lord's vineyard laid waste, and the heathen entered into the sanctuary: and my belly is pained, and my soul in heaviness, because the Lord's people are gone into captivity, and because of the fury of the Lord, and that wind (but neither to fan or to purge) which is coming upon apostate Scotland' (156). Only a person who loved the church could speak so sadly about it.

Yet he did not believe schism was an answer to the church's defects (364), and he deals with this issue in detail in his *Against Separatism*. Rutherford was

---

20   Bonar, *Letters*, p. 15.

committed to working out in corporate and individual life the implications of the headship of Christ over His Church. Connected to this focus is his interest in the faithfulness of the church's ministers, which can be seen in the letters he sent to such, and the Reformed expectation of Christ's presence at the Lord's Supper, which can be deduced from his descriptions of communion occasions (14, 18).

Fifth, Rutherford stresses the significance of covenant theology. He reminds one correspondent: 'Ye come hither to treat with God, and to tryst with Him in His Christ for salvation to your soul, and to seek reconciliation with an angry, wrathful God, in a covenant of peace made to you in Christ' (191). He writes to Christians in Ireland: 'Is it not our comfort, that Christ, the Mediator of the New Covenant, is come betwixt us and God in the business, so that green and young heirs, the like of sinners, have now a Tutor that is God!' (284) For Rutherford, the blessings of the Christian life were the outcome of a covenant relationship with Christ.

Sixth, Rutherford had a deep interest in the anticipated conversion of the Jews. In one letter he says, 'O to see the sight, next to Christ's Coming in the clouds, the most joyful! our elder brethren the Jews and Christ fall upon one another's necks and kiss each other! They have been long asunder; they will be kind to one another when they meet. O day! longed-for and lovely day-dawn! O sweet Jesus, let me see that sight which will be as life from the dead, Thee and Thy ancient people in mutual embraces' (50).

In addition to those doctrines, the letters highlight important aspects of Christian practice. I will mention four features, although others can be identified. *First, for Rutherford, personal holiness was important.* He suggested that Christ should be loved more for giving sanctification than for giving justification because in the former He is remaking His people in His likeness (170). He wrote to one correspondent, 'I recommend mortification to you above everything' (92). To another he wrote, 'I recommend to you holiness and sanctification, and that you keep yourself clean from this present evil world' (213). Yet Rutherford was careful not to be legalistic, for a legal spirit results in pride. He reminded a correspondent that 'the New Covenant seeketh not full measure, nor stented obedience, as the condition of it; because forgiveness hath always place' (249).

Second, the letters reveal the importance of prayer. When he was a pastor in Anwoth, it was his practice to rise at three in the morning to begin the day with study and prayer. In one letter, Rutherford mentions several features of his prayer life: (1) he benefitted by riding alone on a long journey, in giving that time to prayer; (2) he set aside days for prayer and fasting; (3) in praying for others, he got something for himself; (4) because he had experienced God's answers to prayer many times, he used to pray for anything, of how little importance soever. Yet he confesses, 'That the experiences I had of God's hearing me in this and the other particular, being gathered, yet in a new trouble I had always, (once at least,) my faith to seek, as if I were to begin at A B C again' (159).

In addition to personal prayer, Rutherford stressed the value of special seasons of united prayer when 'all who love the truth should join their prayers together, and cry to God with humiliation and fasting' (31). In this letter to Lady Kenmure, he gives several reasons for one such season of prayer: distresses of God's churches abroad, sins and divine judgment in the land, the lamentable and pitiful state of the church, the low spiritual condition of ministers and professing Christians, and that the leaders of the nation and the people turn from evil ways.

He also valued the prayers of others for himself: 'As for myself, I do esteem nothing out of heaven, and next to a communion with Jesus Christ, more to be in the hearts and prayers of the saints' (319). With some believers Rutherford had a prayer-covenant: he wrote to George Gillespie, asking him to 'remember our old covenant and pray for me, and write to me your case' (144).

Third, Rutherford was aware of his personal sinfulness.
He knew from experience 'that known, discovered,
and revealed sins, that are against the conscience, be
eschewed, as most dangerous preparatives to hardness of
heart'. He confessed that 'sudden stirrings of pride, lust,
revenge, love of honours, were not resisted and mourned
for'. He also regretted that 'my grace and gifts bring forth
little or no thankfulness' (159). He also experienced
the disappointing discovery that 'Temptations, that I
supposed to be stricken dead and laid upon their back,
rise again and revive upon me' (92).

Rutherford was astonished that others spoke well
of him and suggested they did so because they did not
know his sins. He wrote to David Dickson: 'I fear that
ye have never known me well. If you saw my inner side,
it is possible that you would pity me, but you would
hardly give me either love or respect: men mistake me
the whole length of the heavens. My sins prevail over
me, and the terror of their guiltiness. I am put often to
ask, if Christ and I did ever shake hands together in
earnest' (168).

*Fourth, Rutherford took into account the likelihood
of opposition for the sake of Christ.* Suffering for Jesus
was not something about which to be ashamed, rather
it is 'the professor's golden garment' (177). To Marion
McNaught, Rutherford wrote, 'Take part with Jesus of
His sufferings, and glory in the marks of Christ' (13).

Concerning her husband, who seemed not to be so committed as she, Rutherford said, 'I will be obliged to him, if he will be willing to suffer for my dear Master' (177). In a letter to John Ewart, he writes, 'I bless His high and glorious name, that the terrors of great men have not affrighted me from openly avouching the Son of God' (134). A possible criticism of Rutherford is that similar strength in facing opposition is not always found in others.

Nevertheless, Rutherford's letters bear testimony that humility, resolve and Christ-centredness do not breed a passionless devotion; rather they result in a devotional life that is marked by passion for Christ, by vibrancy in the spiritual disciplines, that affects every area of life, that loves Christ's church, and looks forward to heaven.

Rutherford was certainly a remarkable man. Gifted by nature, he dedicated all that he was to the service of Jesus Christ. His remarkable ability with words and illustrations, especially seen in his letters, enabled him to compose material of deep insight, profound reverence and lasting impression. The sayings found in this short book are taken from his writings, mainly from his letters. Of course, Rutherford would be disappointed if all we did was marvel at his ingenuity. Rather he would have desired that the readers of his lines in the twenty-first century would respond as did the devout who heard and relished them when they first appeared, and who used them as steps to a deeper understanding of Jesus Christ and His salvation, of His work of grace in the hearts of His people, and of the prospect of being with Him in glory for ever.

Malcolm Maclean

A Collection of Quotes
From
Samuel Rutherford

Jesus and the Gospel

THE FIERY EDGE OF LOVE

1. As long as the Gospel speaks, it ever cries:
   Come, welcome, welcome, sinners, ye will be
   welcome to sup with the Lord.

2. Jesus is saying in the Gospel: 'Come and see.'

3. Christ's offer is really an offer.

4. Christ receives sinners as sinners.

5. There are many heads lying in Christ's bosom,
   but there is room for yours among the rest.

Jesus: His Person and Work

His Incarnation

1. O! What a depth is in it! God and dust married together!

2. Lovely in the womb, the Ancient of Days became young for me.

3. It was not for nothing that our Brother Jesus was an infant.

4. His Father laid the cross on His back, and He carried it thirty-three years, and never gave it a shake to put it off.

His Life and Death

1. What a meek and patient servant Christ was.

2. In everything Christ is excellent.

3. Christ gave as much to God as He desired.

4. Christ took on Him the guilt of our sin, that is, the actual obligation to be punished for sin.

5. Not a penny that sinners took from God, but Christ restored a pound for it again.

6. 'I thirst.' O wells! O lochs! O running streams! Where were you all when my Lord could not get a drink?

His Resurrection, Ascension and Second Coming

1. The Lord, in His resurrection, has triumphed over death and hell, and delivered His elect people from this grievous curse.

2. Glory, glory to our King! Long may He wear His crown!

3. Christ is under covenant to enjoy His reward when He hath done His work.

4. Christ's undertaking as High Priest, Advocate and Intercessor is to carry on and perfect as Mediator all that are given to Him of the Father.

5. Who knows . . . what motions of compassion
   are in the man Christ now in heaven?

6. Christ is disposed to give grace as a river.

7. Ponder the glory of a crucified, risen and
   ascended Redeemer.

8. That must be a glad meeting for evermore,
   when we shall meet with the Bridegroom.

9. Sigh and long for the dawning of that
   morning, and the breaking of that day, of the
   Coming of the Son of Man, when the shadows
   shall flee away.

Communion with Jesus

1. I must give over all attempt to fathom the depth of His love.

2. Christ will spare no pains to gain His own.

3. There is more love in Christ than angels and men could fathom.

4. I would seek no more to make me happy for evermore but a thorough and clear sight of the beauty of Jesus, my Lord.

5. The King hath led me up to a measure of joy and communion with my Bridegroom that I never attained to before.

6. I have the company of a Lord who can teach us all to be kind.

7. My debt to the love of Christ [shall] lie unpaid for all eternity.

8. There is more to be had in Christ in this life than I believed.

9. I am pained with wondering at new-opened treasures in Christ.

10. How happy were I to see the coronation day of Christ!

11. I would not exchange my Lord Jesus with all the comfort out of heaven.

12. Christ is our sweet Nightingale, that in the time of the Gospel sings sweetly.

13. Let me have no joy but the warmness and fire of Christ's love; I seek no other, God knoweth.

14. Christ hath come and run away to heaven with my heart and my love, so that neither heart nor love is mine.

15. O for love to Him who is altogether lovely!

16. Oh, if I could yoke in amongst the thick of angels, and seraphims, and now glorified saints, and could raise a new love-song of Christ, before all the world!

God

His Covenant

1. The Father and Christ transacted a bargain from eternity concerning thee, by name.

2. This covenant was manifested in time, but it was transacted from eternity.

3. We come to the knowledge of our election to glory by believing.

4. The book of life must be a huge volume!

5. He must of necessity, from His redeeming love and election in the covenant of redemption, bring them all in.

6. The decree is: 'Whoever believes is mine.' Amen, dear Jesus.

His Grace

1. Every act of grace in God is an act of omnipotence.

2. Grace is mercy given for nothing.

3. O, it be a hard matter to persuade nature what grace is!

4. The weakest measure of saving grace is stronger than the highest measure of malice.

5. It is grace that holds us up that we fall not.

His Mercy

1. Mercy flows not from God essentially, but of mere grace.

2. God's mercy is a great net; all the fish that come in the net are brought to land.

His Providence

1. The great Master Gardener, the Father of our Lord Jesus Christ, in a wonderful providence, with His own hand planted me here, where by His grace in this part of His vineyard I grow.

2. God's dispensation is spotless, yet it is not Scripture to me.

3. I adore and kiss the providence of my Lord, who knoweth well what is most expedient for me.

Christian Living

Affections

1. Affections are the feet of the soul.

2. Affections leap out and embrace Christ.

3. When the affections are lame, the soul moves on crutches.

4. When there is any corruption in the affections, it stagnates the soul, will, mind and conscience.

Conscience

1. The Word of God must be the rule of conscience.

2. Hurt not your conscience with any known sin.

3. It is a mark of conscience in a right frame to be affected with a sense of the least sin.

4. See that ye keep your consciences void of offence towards God and man.

5.   Whatever ye do, keep the conscience whole.

6.   Keep your conscience clean and undefiled.

7.   A soul that is truly sanctified will be loathe to make a hole in his neighbour's conscience, that he may see what is there.

Faith

1.   Faith is exceeding charitable, and believeth no evil of God.

2.   The wisdom of faith knoweth a shop where there is a more excellent suit of clothes for the soul.

3.   Faith cannot be but loving and kind to Christ.

4.   Faith will teach you to kiss a striking Lord.

5.   The least faith doth justify, but the Gospel requireth a growth in faith.

6.   Faith grips the promises.

7. The smallest measure of faith is sincere adherence to Christ.

8. A little faith is faith.

Love

1. Love is the fire of our obedience.

2. Love hath broad shoulders, and will bear many things.

3. Sufferings blunt not the fiery edge of love.

4. Gracious love produceth love-sickness.

5. Love and longing for Christ have eagle's wings.

6. Love flieth when words do but creep as a snail.

Humility

1. Humble sinners have high thoughts of free grace.

2.   Think little of thyself, and thou art within
sight of Christ.

3.   The Lord gives unto the humbled sinner a
high place and seat in heaven.

4.   It is a great matter to be humbled and yet to
believe, both at one time.

5.   The lowly man is Christ's friend.

Prayer

1.   God loves a hungry child that's aye [always]
crying for bread.

2.   Christ often hears when He doth not answer;
His not answering is an answer.

3.   Prayer can reach as far as omnipotence.

4.   Prayer puts God on noble acts of
omnipotence.

5.   The sweetest communion that Christ seeks of
us on earth is prayer.

6. I think it is easy to get anything from the King by prayer, and to use holy violence with Him.

7. Hold fast thy grip of the Lord, and pray to Him to hold His grip fast on you.

Repentance and Holiness

1. Repentance is a work of the Gospel and not a work of the law.

2. Repentance and rising by the grace of God out of the state of sin is better than all the civility and Pharisaical righteousness in the world.

3. To mourn for sin is a grace promised under the New Testament.

4. Justified persons are to pray for pardon of confessed sins.

5. Every one of us should take to heart our own sins, and be humbled before God for them.

6. The old ashes of my sins are a new fire to my sorrow.

7. I am a deeper hypocrite and shallower professor than every one believeth.

8. Justification removeth not the indwelling of sin.

9. I recommend mortification to you above anything.

10. Christ in one saint cannot be cruel to Christ in another saint.

11. True honour is to be great in the sight of God.

Christian Service

Christian Witness

1. We owe to our royal King and princely Master a testimony.

2. I seek no other thing than that my Lord may be honoured by me in giving a testimony.

3. Loving friend, I earnestly desire your salvation.

4. Take as many to heaven with you as ye are able to draw.

5. The more ye draw with you, ye shall be the welcome yourself.

6. I commend Christ to you as the Staff of your old age.

7. None is so kind as my royal King and Master.

8. They are not worthy of Jesus who will not take a blow for their Master's sake.

Preaching

1. The Lord knoweth that I preferred preaching of Christ, and still do, to anything, next to Christ Himself.

2. There is nothing out of heaven, next to Christ, dearer to me than my ministry.

3. Alas, that I cannot draw souls and Christ together!

4. Oh, how blessed a thing is it to labour for Christ!

5. I fear I have done little good in my ministry.

6. I have received many ... dashes and heavy strokes since the Lord called me to the ministry.

7. I have many a grieved heart daily in my calling.

8. What are ministers but earthen pitchers carrying the heavenly treasures?

9. Ministers ... are but the Bridegroom's friends carrying your love letters from your Husband.

Fighting the Devil

1. We have a greater victory over Satan than we know.

2. The devil is but God's master fencer, to teach us to handle our weapons.

3. Blessed are they who, in the wisdom of God's Spirit, can pull the mask off the devil and sin; see the devil to be the devil, and sin to be sin.

4. Faith is more assaulted than any other grace; Satan shaketh other graces, but this is winnowed between heaven and earth.

5. We are not ... to usurp the devil's office, to accuse a brother.

Avoiding the World

1.   The world is the devil's great trawling net, that has taken thousands and slain them.

2.   The foolish worldlings buy the world before ever they take a good sight of it.

3.   It is a dangerous thing once to let the world into our heart.

4.   Oh, how heavenly a thing it is to be dead, and dumb, and deaf to this world's sweet music!

Carrying His Cross

1.   The weightiest end of the cross of Christ that is laid upon you lieth upon your strong Saviour.

2.   Be patient: Christ went to heaven with many a wrong.

3.   I am not ashamed of His cross.

4. The shame of Christ's cross shall not be my shame.

5. His cross is the sweetest burden I bare.

6. I take His cross in my arms with joy. It is such a burden as wings are to a bird, or sails are to a ship.

Suffering for Christ

1. They are blessed who suffer and sin not, for suffering is the badge that Christ hath put upon His followers.

2. Let us be glad and rejoice that we have blood, losses and wounds to show our Master and Captain at His appearance, and what we suffered for His cause.

3. Not one grain-weight more is laid on me than He hath enabled me to bear.

4. Come all crosses, welcome, welcome, so that I may get my heartful of my Lord Jesus.

5. O, what owe I to the file, to the hammer, to the furnace of my Lord Jesus!

6. I hope to lose nothing in this furnace but dross.

7. It is Christ's truth I now suffer for.

8. I am filled with joy in my sufferings.

9. Glorify the Lord in your sufferings, and take His banner of love, and spread it over you.

10. I know that an afflicted life looks very like the way that leads to the kingdom.

The Church

1. So long as God hath a vineyard there will be foxes in it to destroy the vines.

2. Woe unto us for these sad divisions that make us lose the fair scent of the Rose of Sharon.

3. An afflicted church is a praying church.

4. Think not much of a storm upon the ship that Christ saileth in; there shall no passenger fall overboard; but the crazed ship and the sea-sick passenger shall come to land.

Thinking of Heaven

1. The sea-sick passenger shall come to land; Christ will be the first that will meet you on the shore.

2. If you knew the welcome that waits for you when you come home, you would hasten your pace.

3. Stoop, stoop! It is a low entry to go in at heaven's gates.

4. There is much humility in heaven.

5. We shall see many in heaven whom we judged to be castaways.

6. Many go to heaven with you, and you hear not the sound of their feet in their journey.

7. It is impossible that a man can take his lusts to heaven with him.

8. Think you it a small honour to stand before the throne of God and the Lamb?

9. He would have us flying to heaven, and we are still creeping upon this earth.

10. I owe my heaven to Christ.

11. It is the sweeter that no napkin, but His own immediate hand, shall wipe my sinful face.

12. O for the long day, and the high sun, and the fair garden, and the King's great city up above these visible heavens!

13. I rejoice in the hope of that glory to be revealed.

14. I am a faint, dead-hearted, cowardly man, oft borne down and hungry in waiting for the marriage-supper of the Lamb.

15. Sure I am, He is the best half of heaven.

Eternity and Time

1. Eternity is a great word, but the thing itself is greater.

2. This life is nothing in comparison of eternity.

3. O for a sight of eternity's glory!

4. O for eternity's leisure to look on Him.

5. O time, time, go swiftly, and hasten that day!

6. O time, time, flee swiftly, that our communion with Jesus may be perfected.

A Letter from Rutherford

To my Lady Kenmure,[1]

Madam,

I have longed exceedingly to hear of your life and health, and growth in the grace of God. I lacked the opportunity of a bearer, in respect I did not understand of the hasty departure of the last, by whom I might have saluted your Ladyship, and therefore I could not write before this time. I entreat you, Madam, let me have two lines from you concerning your present condition. I know ye are in grief and heaviness; and if it were not so, ye might be afraid, because then your way should not be so like the way that (our Lord saith) leadeth to the New Jerusalem. Sure I am, if ye knew what were before you, or if ye saw but some glances of it, ye would with gladness swim through the present floods of sorrow, spreading forth your arms out of desire to be at land. If God have given you the Earnest of the Spirit, as part of payment of God's principal sum, ye have to rejoice; for our Lord will not lose

---

1.   Lady Kenmure was previously Lady Jane Campbell, the third daughter of the Duke of Argyll. Rutherford wrote to her regularly and after his death in 1661 she provided help for his widow and daughter. He wrote this letter in February 1630 from Anwoth. In 1634, her first husband died and Rutherford described what occurred in his book, *The Last and Heavenly Speeches and Glorious Departure of John Viscount Kenmure*, which was published in 1649.

His earnest, neither will He go back or repent Him of the bargain. If ye find at some time a longing to see God, joy in the assurance of that sight, howbeit that feast be but like the Passover, that cometh about only once a year. Peace of conscience, liberty of prayer, the doors of God's treasure cast up to the soul, and a clear sight of Himself looking out, and saying, with a smiling countenance, 'Welcome to Me, afflicted soul;' this is the earnest that He giveth sometimes, and which maketh glad the heart, and is an evidence that the bargain will hold. But to the end ye may get this earnest, it were good to come oft into terms of speech with God, both in prayer and hearing of the Word. For this is the house of wine, where ye meet with your Well-Beloved. Here it is where He kisseth you with the kisses of His mouth, and where ye feel the smell of His garments; and they have indeed a most fragrant and glorious smell. Ye must, I say, wait upon Him, and be often communing with Him, whose lips are as lilies, dropping sweet-smelling myrrh, and by the moving thereof He will assuage your grief; for the Christ that saveth you is a speaking Christ; the church knoweth Him by His voice (Song 2:8), and can discern His tongue amongst a thousand. I say this to the end ye should not love those dumb masks of antichristian ceremonies, that the church[2] where

2. Episcopal services had been imposed.

ye are for a time hath cast over the Christ whom your soul loveth. This is to set before you a dumb Christ. But when our Lord cometh, He speaketh to the heart in the simplicity of the Gospel.

I have neither tongue nor pen to express to you the happiness of such as are in Christ. When ye have sold all that ye have, and bought the field wherein this pearl is, ye will think it no bad market; for if ye be in Him, all His is yours, and ye are in Him; therefore, 'because He liveth, ye shall live also' (John 14:19). And what is that else, but as if the Son had said, 'I will not have heaven except My redeemed ones be with Me: they and I cannot live asunder. Abide in Me, and I in you.' O sweet communion, when Christ and we are through-other,[3] and are no longer two! 'Father, I will that those whom Thou hast given Me be with Me where I am, to behold My glory that Thou hast given Me' (John 17:24). Amen, dear Jesus, let it be according to that word. I wonder that ever your heart should be cast down, if ye believe this truth. I and they are not worthy of Jesus Christ, who will not suffer forty years' trouble for Him, since they have such glorious promises. But we fools believe those promises as the man that read Plato's writings concerning the immortality of the soul: so long as the book was in his hand he believed all was true, and that the soul could not

---

3.   Mixed up with each other.

die; but so soon as he laid by the book, he began to imagine that the soul is but a smoke or airy vapour, that perisheth with the expiring of the breath. So we at starts do assent to the sweet and precious promises; but, laying aside God's book, we begin to call all in question. It is faith indeed to believe without a pledge, and to hold the heart constant at this work; and when we doubt, to run to the Law and to the Testimony, and stay there. Madam, hold you here: here is your Father's testament – read it; in it He hath left to you remission of sins and life everlasting. If all that ye have here be crosses and troubles, down-castings, frequent desertions, and departure of the Lord, who is suiting you in marriage, courage! He who is wooer and suitor should not be an household man with you till ye and He come up to His Father's house together. He purposeth to do you good at your latter end (Deut. 8:16), and to give you rest from the days of adversity (Ps. 94:13). 'It is good to bear the yoke of God in your youth' (Lam. 3:27). 'Turn in to your stronghold as a prisoner of hope' (Zech. 9:12). 'For the vision is for an appointed time; but at the end it shall speak, and not lie: though it tarry, wait for it, because it will surely come, it will not tarry' (Hab. 2:3). Hear Himself saying, 'Come, My people' (rejoice, He calleth on you!), 'enter thou into thy chambers, and shut thy doors about thee; hide thyself, as it were for a little moment, till the indignation be past' (Isa. 26:20). Believe, then, believe and be saved; think not hard if ye get not your will, nor your delights in this life; God will have you to rejoice in nothing but Himself. God forbid that ye should rejoice in anything but in the cross of Christ (Gal. 6:14).

Our church, Madam, is decaying – she is like Ephraim's cake (Hos. 7:9); 'and grey hairs are here and there upon her, and she knoweth it not.' She is old and grey-haired, near the grave, and no man taketh it to heart. Her wine is sour and is corrupted. Now if Phinehas' wife did live she might travail in birth and die, to see the ark of God taken, and the glory depart from our Israel. The power and life of religion is away. 'Woe be to us! for the day goeth away, for the shadows of the evening are stretched out' (Jer. 6:4). Madam, Zion is the ship wherein ye are carried to Canaan; if she suffer shipwreck, ye will be cast overboard upon death and life, to swim to land upon broken boards. It were time for us, by prayer, to put upon our master-pilot, Jesus, and to cry, 'Master, save us; we perish.' Grace, grace be with you. We would think it a blessing to our kirk to see you here; but our sins withhold good things from us. The great Messenger of the Covenant preserve you in body and spirit.

Yours in the Lord,
S.R.

SELECTED BIBLIOGRAPHY

LIST OF RUTHERFORD'S WRITINGS

1636   *Exercitationes Apologeticae pro Divina Gratia*

1642   *A Peaceable and Temperate Plea for Paul's Presbytery in Scotland*

1644   *The Due Right of Presbyteries*

        Lex, Rex

1645   *The Trial and Triumph of Faith* (sermons on Jesus and the Canaanite woman described in Matthew and Mark)

1646   *The Divine Right of Church Government and Excommunication,* including *A Dispute touching Scandal and Christian Liberty*

1647   *Christ Dying and Drawing Sinners to Himself* (sermons on John 12:27-33)

1648   *A Survey of the Spiritual Antichrist*, including a
        pamphlet called *A Modest Survey of the Secrets
        of Antinomianism*.

1649   *A Free Disputation against Pretended Liberty of
        Conscience*

        *The Last and Heavenly Speeches of John Gordon,
        Viscount Kenmure*

1651   *Disputatio Scholastica de Divina Providentia*

1655   *The Covenant of Life Opened*

1658   *A Survey of the Survey of that Sum of Church
        Discipline*

1659   *Influences of the Life of Grace*

POSTHUMOUS PUBLICATIONS

1668   *An Examination of Arminianism*, based
        on material Rutherford had prepared in
        St Andrews, was published in Holland in 1668.

1713   *A Treatise on Prayer: The Power and Prevalency
        of Faith and Prayer*.

1738   *The Cruel Watchmen* (also found in *Quaint
        Sermons by Samuel Rutherford* but called 'The
        Church Seeking her Lord').

COLLECTIONS OF SERMONS BY RUTHERFORD

1877   *Fourteen Communion Sermons*, edited by Andrew A. Bonar. These sermons had been published previously, with twelve in a volume edited by Bonar called *Twelve Communion Sermons* (1876).

1885   *Quaint Sermons by Samuel Rutherford*, edited by Andrew A. Bonar. These eighteen sermons were selected from a manuscript of notes of previously unpublished sermons.

OTHER MATERIAL BY RUTHERFORD

A catechism by Rutherford was published in A. F. Mitchell (1886), *Catechisms of the Second Reformation*, Nisbet.

Andrew Bonar, *Letters of Samuel Rutherford* (with a sketch of his life and biographical notices of his correspondents), Oliphant, Anderson and Ferrier.

BIOGRAPHIES OF RUTHERFORD

A. Taylor Innes (1892), 'Samuel Rutherfurd,' in *Studies in Scottish History*, Hodder and Stoughton.

Robert Gilmour (1904), *Samuel Rutherford*, Oliphant, Anderson and Ferrier.

Marcus Loane (2009), 'Samuel Rutherford,' in *Makers of Puritan History*, Banner of Truth.

Thomas Murray (1828), *Life of Samuel Rutherford*, William Oliphant.

Andrew Thomson (1885), *Samuel Rutherford*, Hodder and Stoughton.

Alexander Whyte (1894), *Samuel Rutherford and his Correspondents*, Oliphant, Anderson and Ferrier.

Christian Focus Publications

Our mission statement –

STAYING FAITHFUL

In dependence upon God we seek to impact the world through literature faithful to His infallible Word, the Bible. Our aim is to ensure that the Lord Jesus Christ is presented as the only hope to obtain forgiveness of sin, live a useful life and look forward to heaven with Him.

Our books are published in four imprints:

CHRISTIAN
FOCUS

Popular works including biographies, commentaries, basic doctrine and Christian living.

CHRISTIAN
HERITAGE

Books representing some of the best material from the rich heritage of the church.

MENTOR

Books written at a level suitable for Bible College and seminary students, pastors, and other serious readers. The imprint includes commentaries, doctrinal studies, examination of current issues and church history.

CF4•K

Children's books for quality Bible teaching and for all age groups: Sunday school curriculum, puzzle and activity books; personal and family devotional titles, biographies and inspirational stories — because you are never too young to know Jesus!

Christian Focus Publications Ltd,
Geanies House, Fearn, Ross-shire,
IV20 1TW, Scotland, United Kingdom.
www.christianfocus.com
blog.christianfocus.com